Excitable
beast of
burden

Attractive green
complexion

Waistcoat made
from alligator
skin

Once upon a
time this top
was white!

SHREK

THE ESSENTIAL GUIDE

Written by Stephen Cole

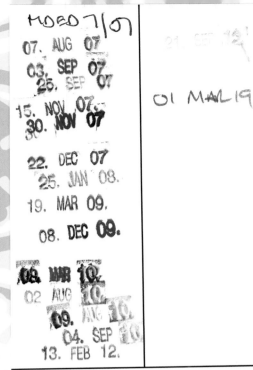

Contents

Once upon a time...

There was a large green ogre who became a great hero... a small donkey who became his noble steed... and a beautiful princess who kept a mysterious secret.

This is their story...

Publisher's note: Please do not use pages from this book as toilet paper. This may impair your enjoyment of the tale.

Shrek

At first glance, Shrek might appear to be a big, green, terrifying ogre. But there's much more to Shrek than meets the eye. He may look scary, but really he's a kind ogre with a very big heart. He used to live alone in a swamp but that all changed when he met Princess Fiona. They had a lot more in common than they first realized!

Resourceful ogres use their vast quantities of ear wax to make candles.

Alligator-skin waistcoat.

Tartan trousers – Shrek comes from a very old family of McOgres.

Extra-large leather shoes made to withstand Shrek's rancid feet.

Great outdoors

Shrek loves nature and especially his swamp home. He gives it all up when he marries Fiona and moves to Far Far Away. However, when royal duties are getting him down he dreams of the days when all he had to think about was whether to have slug or bug for dinner.

Normally Shrek is the scarer not the scaree. However, when Fiona tells Shrek she is pregnant, he has awful nightmares about hundreds of babies taking over his swamp house. Even Donkey and Puss turn into mini-Shreks!

To keep his clothes damp and covered in mildew, Shrek soaks them in stagnant swamp water and then leaves them in the shade to fester.

Whirlwind adventures!

Shrek used to think he was a real loner. But that was before he formed a firm friendship with Donkey and Puss In Boots. Now he knows that some people get under your skin – even if they get on your nerves at the same time!

Shrek's shoulder makes a handy seat for for his feline friend.

Eyes agleam at the thought of a great adventure ahead

Fight for your rights!

Whether it's hundreds of foolish knaves or villains from the The Poison Apple, Shrek has always had to defend himself.

Boiled giant slug

Pumpkin stuffed with worms

Slimy eyeballs

Fish-eye tartare with squashed bugs

Dead skin flakes for seasoning

Shrek's favourite foods

Shrek's appetite is bad news for swamp life!

• He catches weedrats and roasts them over an open fire! They're also very good in stews.

• Wart-covered swamp toads are another favourite – they're especially nice in soup!

• If Shrek gets peckish after his meal, he likes to snack on eyeballs on toast – scrumptious!

Shrek's Swamp

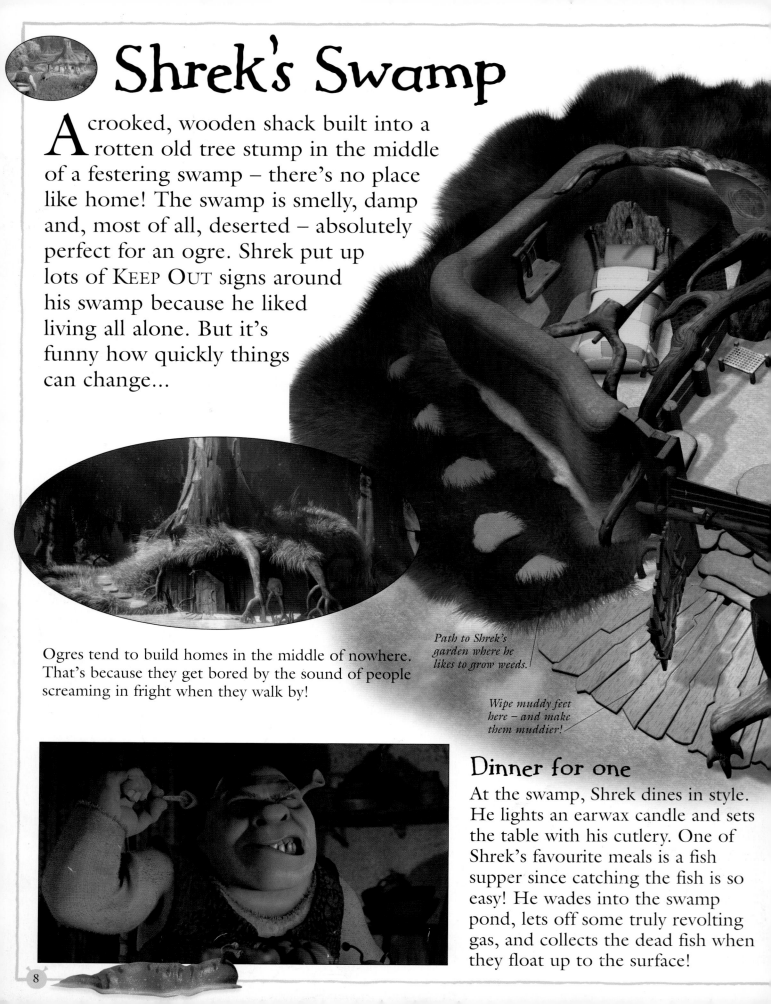

A crooked, wooden shack built into a rotten old tree stump in the middle of a festering swamp – there's no place like home! The swamp is smelly, damp and, most of all, deserted – absolutely perfect for an ogre. Shrek put up lots of KEEP OUT signs around his swamp because he liked living all alone. But it's funny how quickly things can change...

Ogres tend to build homes in the middle of nowhere. That's because they get bored by the sound of people screaming in fright when they walk by!

Path to Shrek's garden where he likes to grow weeds.

Wipe muddy feet here – and make them muddier!

Dinner for one

At the swamp, Shrek dines in style. He lights an earwax candle and sets the table with his cutlery. One of Shrek's favourite meals is a fish supper since catching the fish is so easy! He wades into the swamp pond, lets off some truly revolting gas, and collects the dead fish when they float up to the surface!

Barrel of home-
brewed ogre ale.

Firewood gathered
by smashing up
tree-trunks.

All ogre cooking
is done over an
open fire.

Shrek loves a slimy mud
shower to wake him up
in the morning. All that
gloopy muck is
great as a
mouthwash
as well!

Water trough (also
good for bathing feet).

Antique
rottenwood
dining table.

Window for
checking no
one comes near.

Reinforced chair
to hold Shrek's
weight.

Far-out(side) toilet

Ogres keep their toilets outside for a
good reason. The build-up of smelly
ogre gases *indoors* could pose a
serious health risk! Since swamps
smell so bad anyway, no one really
notices the extra stink outside…

For toilet paper, Shrek rips out
pages from a silly old fairy-tale book.
He never dreams that fairy-tale
magic will one day touch *his* life
for real!

The toilet's rickety
construction is good
for ventilation.

Tree house!

Living in the stump of an old tree
has lots to recommend it. The roots
are incredibly strong, so the house
has good foundations, and the thick
turf roof helps to keep the house
cool in summer and warm in winter.
No wonder a stump is home from
home for an ogre!

Donkey

This hip-talking, fast-walking, lucky, plucky donkey charges straight into Shrek and Shrek's world becomes a lot louder! Donkey loves to be involved in everything and, though he may not admit it, Shrek wouldn't be without him. Now that Donkey is a dad, maybe he'll calm down – or maybe not!

Long ears droop when sad and perk up when happy.

Who could resist such soulful brown eyes?

Wide awake

When Shrek has to take on royal duties, Donkey and Puss In Boots become Shrek's administrative assistants. They make sure he wakes on time, knows which functions he must attend and carries out his tasks correctly – well, two out of three isn't bad. Still, Donkey is ever positive. After a disastrous day of duties, Donkey declares, 'I think that went pretty well.'

Loud and proud!

• Donkey's ability to talk often surprises the people he meets. But as Shrek puts it, 'It's getting him to shut up that's the trick!'

• He's prone to blind panic – about the only thing that doesn't scare him stupid is Shrek!

• He loves to sing, wail, and whistle – or do anything that involves lots of noise.

Red hot love!

This smooth-talking donkey doesn't care about looks. In fact, he sometimes gets carried away – not just by romance, but by his enormous fire-breathing dragon girlfriend!

Donkey dad

What do you get when you cross a dragon with a donkey? Lots and lots of flying, fire-breathing DRONKEYS! Donkey loves being a dad, and he gives his kids cool names like Peanut, Coco, Parfait, Bananas and Debbie!

Princess Fiona

After falling victim to a magical enchantment as a small girl, the beautiful Princess Fiona was sent by her parents to a far-off tower to await rescue by a handsome prince. When her rescuer turned out to be a green ogre called Shrek, fiesty Fiona realised that she no longer had to hide her secret. As the pair fall in love, Fiona starts to love her green skin.

Fiona finds Shrek as charming as any prince. You know it's true love when you try to out-belch each other!

An unorthodox rescue

When her parents locked her in a tower, Fiona expected to be rescued by her prince charming. Instead, she got a green ogre who breaks all the rules! Rather than waking her with a kiss, he shook her by the shoulders. And when she gave him her delicate hanky as a token of gratitude, he wiped his sooty face with it! Their marriage is just as unconventional.

The Princess Diaries

As a child, Fiona kept a diary full of her dreams of fairy tale happiness. Since then she's learned one or two home truths...

• A good man is hard to find – especially when he's been burnt to a crisp by a dragon while trying to rescue you!

• Prince Charming is not charming at all!

• Your true love could be the most unlikely candidate!

Ponytail doubles as wicked weapon in martial arts combat!

Flat comfortable slippers – much more practical than Cinderella's delicate glass ones.

Royal dress designed with high kicks in mind.

Beware of imposters!

At the royal ball in Far Far Away, Prince Charming tried to convince Fiona that he was Shrek, transformed by a magic potion. It didn't take Fiona long to realise that there was nothing magical at all about the pompous pretender by her side!

Baby talk

A lot has happened since Fiona and Shrek were newlyweds, living a peaceful life in their swamp. Fiona has some exciting news that will change their lives forever. As Shrek embarks on a voyage to find Artie, Fiona tells him that they are going to be parents!

Fairy-tale Squatters

Shrek got quite a shock when he discovered hundreds of fairy-tale characters camping out in his swamp! Lord Farquaad, fed up with magical folk lowering the tone of his perfect kingdom, had them all chucked out. With no place to go, the fairy-tale folk packed up their troubles – and dumped them right at Shrek's door!

Witches and wizards don't usually mix – they always argue over whose hat is pointiest.

Character Key

1 Grand Wizard

2 Straw House Pig

3 Tom Thumb

4 Shoemaker's Elf

5 Leprechaun

6 Children of the Shoe

7 Trainee Wizard

8 Bashful Dwarf

9 Happy Dwarf

10 Brick & Stick Pigs

Shrek likes his privacy – he didn't want squatters on his land!

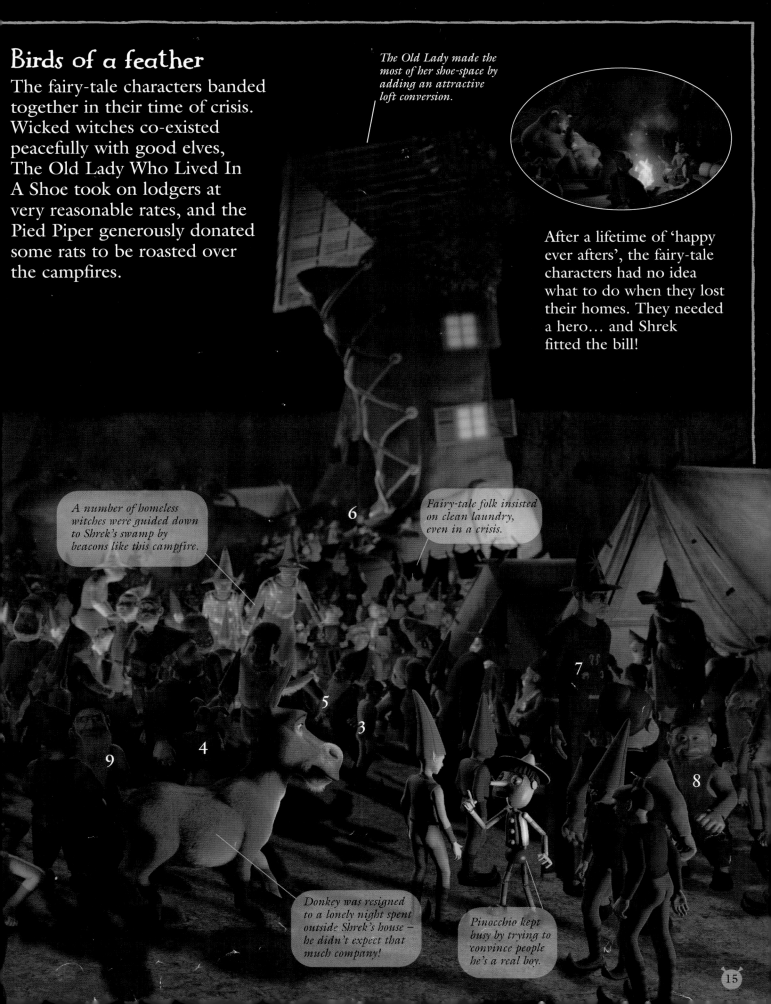

Birds of a feather

The fairy-tale characters banded together in their time of crisis. Wicked witches co-existed peacefully with good elves, The Old Lady Who Lived In A Shoe took on lodgers at very reasonable rates, and the Pied Piper generously donated some rats to be roasted over the campfires.

The Old Lady made the most of her shoe-space by adding an attractive loft conversion.

After a lifetime of 'happy ever afters', the fairy-tale characters had no idea what to do when they lost their homes. They needed a hero… and Shrek fitted the bill!

A number of homeless witches were guided down to Shrek's swamp by beacons like this campfire.

Fairy-tale folk insisted on clean laundry, even in a crisis.

6

7

5

3

4

9

8

Donkey was resigned to a lonely night spent outside Shrek's house – he didn't expect that much company!

Pinocchio kept busy by trying to convince people he's a real boy.

Happy Ever After?

Gingy had never seen a fairy – until he met a dazzling fairy at the Far Far Away ball.

Elves, unicorns, fairies, witches, a whole truckload of talking animals… it looked like there'd be no fairy-tale ending for these magical characters, forced by Farquaad to live in Shrek's swamp! The grumpy ogre didn't want them on his land, and set out to have them removed. But once his adventures had softened his heart just a little, Shrek realised that fairy-tale company could actually be fun – and now he lets them visit whenever they like!

Three Little Pigs

Shrek used to find the pigs and their squealing grating. But when you're being pursued by a rabble of rogues, you have to take help where you can find it. Raising their pinkies as they sip their tea, the pigs tell Charming and his henchmen that they have never even heard of Shrek or Fiona.

Bread to leave trail of crumbs

Fascinating fairy-tale facts

• Hansel and Gretel have real sweet teeth – they even eat the sugar windows of the witch's house.

• The big bad wolf wears old ladies' clothes even when he's *not* trying to eat Red Riding Hood.

• The Three Little Pigs stay on strict diets to make sure they *remain* little.

• Tom Thumb and Thumbelina like nothing more than a buffet of finger food.

The Big Bad Wolf

An old-fashioned wolf, he sticks to the tricks he knows: dress up like an old woman and blow down pigs' houses before they master the art of cement-mixing. Everyone's wise to his tricks, but the wolf doesn't care – he prefers to take it easy all day in other people's beds!

The townspeople of Duloc rounded up the local dwarves and handed them over to Farquaad's guards in exhange for gold.

Grandma's nightdress.

It's safer to sit on a wolf than get near the farmer's wife.

Wooden head (no puppet strings attached).

The pigs helpfully wear hats so they can be told apart. This one wears a hard hat inside his house of bricks.

This pig sticks with a house made of twigs. He's no stranger to homelessness.

Losing his flimsy home is never the final straw for this little pig.

Gingy

The Gingerbread Man may look soft and sweet, but in fact he is one tough cookie! When the chocolate chips are down, he's ginger-*bred* to be a sweet friend who can always be relied on! Whether being tortured by Lord Farquaad or threatened by Captain Hook, Gingy never gives his friends and fellow fairy-tale creatures away!

Super-special gumdrop buttons – fashionable and delicious.

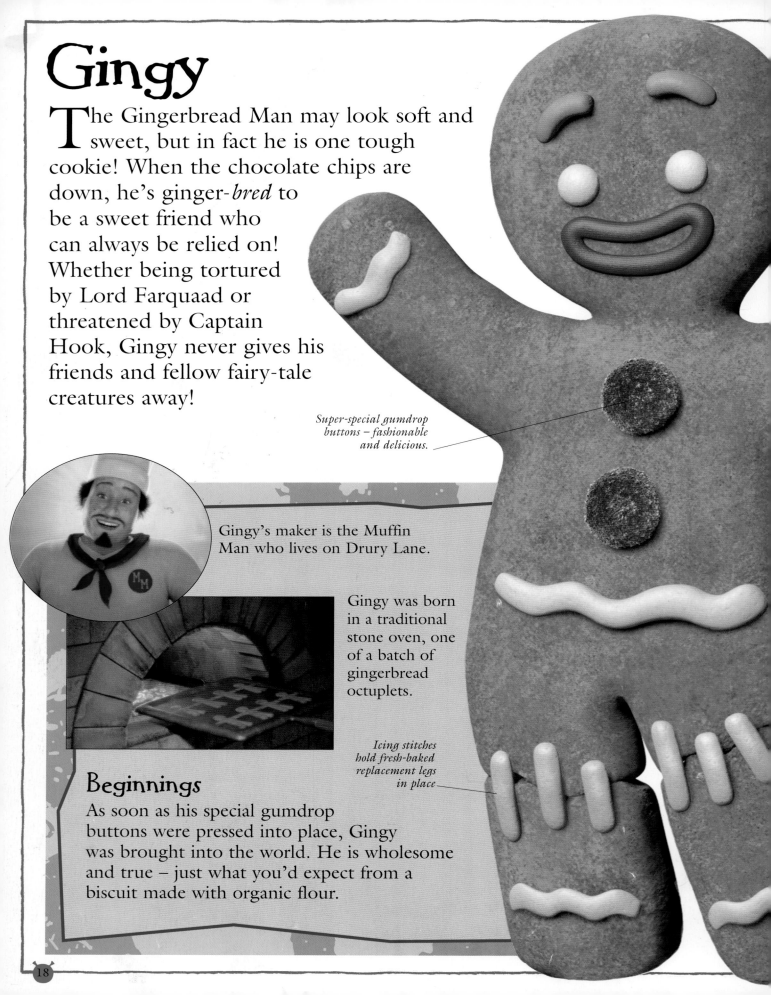

Gingy's maker is the Muffin Man who lives on Drury Lane.

Gingy was born in a traditional stone oven, one of a batch of gingerbread octuplets.

Icing stitches hold fresh-baked replacement legs in place

Beginnings

As soon as his special gumdrop buttons were pressed into place, Gingy was brought into the world. He is wholesome and true – just what you'd expect from a biscuit made with organic flour.

Bread for speed!

Gingy is a super-fast runner – as the old rhyme goes, "You can't catch me, I'm the Gingerbread Man!" This natural speed and agility is rare in the cookie-based community. Gingy puts his special skill down to hard work and brilliant baking.

Few people realise that a gingerbread man's icing is as distinctive among biscuits as fingerprints are among humans.

Mongo

When Shrek needed some serious cookie muscle to rescue Fiona, Gingy got in touch with the Muffin Man. The result was Mongo, a giant gingerbread brute whose strength and limited intelligence made him ideal for the mission Shrek had planned!

In the face of danger, Gingy is a courageous cookie who doesn't crumble!

Sweet memories

When faced with torture at the hands of Charming and Captain Hook, Gingy's whole life flashes before him...

• Young Gingy went to the Cookie Academy where he excelled at Home Economics.

• Gingy's wedding day was blissfully happy. But sadly, the relationship soon went stale and crumbled.

• Having lost both his legs following a cruel dunking in milk at the hands of Farquaad, Gingy needed new limbs. State-of-the-art icing let cookie surgeons transplant two fresh legs. After months of painful exercise and rehabilitation, Gingy's new legs were as strong as the old set.

Pinocchio

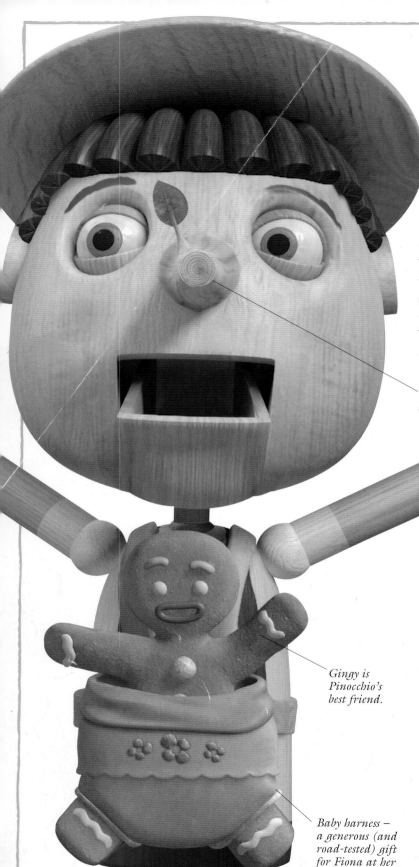

To caring, sharing Pinocchio, honesty is very important. If he tells a fib, his nose grows as long as a flagpole and gives him away! He is a carved puppet who longs to be a real boy. He may be made of wood but his loving, kind heart is anything *but* wooden!

Pinocchio never finds it hard to turn over a new leaf.

Stylishly articulated fingers.

Super-smooth arms – "plane" to see.

Gingy is Pinocchio's best friend.

Baby harness – a generous (and road-tested) gift for Fiona at her baby shower.

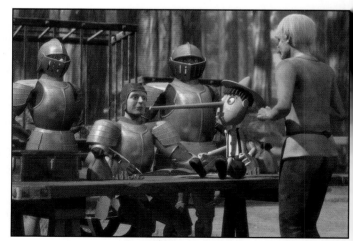

Father's day

When the old man who carved Pinocchio sold him to Lord Farquaad's guards for a measly five shillings, he tried to insist he was a real boy and not a wooden puppet. Sadly, as he stretched the truth, his nose stretched too!

Man and (wooden) boy

Pinocchio and Gingy are the best of fairy-tale friends, and they're also good pals to Shrek. When Shrek left the swamp to go to Far Far Away, they helped housesit for him. And when they learned he was in trouble, the pair led the charge to save him – in unique and daring style!

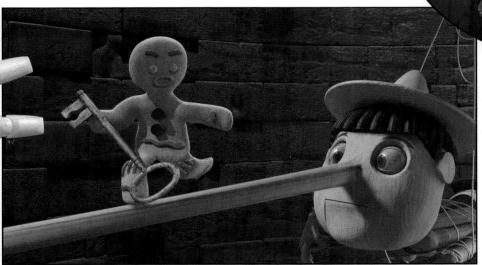

Pinocchio's nose played a vital part in rescuing Shrek from prison. By denying he was wearing ladies' underwear when he actually was, Pinocchio's telescopic snoot stretched all the way over to Shrek's manacles – allowing Gingy to zip across and set the ogre free!

Pinocchio gets even more red-cheeked when under pressure.

This boy-toy sure can boogie!

Fast-talker

There's only one way that Pinocchio can talk his way out of trouble – with extreme difficulty! For example...

Charming: So tell me puppet ... Where is Shrek?
Pinocchio: Well, I don't know where he's not.
C: You're telling me you don't know where Shrek is?
P: It wouldn't be inaccurate to assume that I couldn't exactly not say that is or isn't almost partially incorrect.
C: So you do know where he is!
P: On the contrary, I'm possibly, more or less, not definitely, rejecting the idea that in no way, with any amount of uncertainty that...

Not one to shy away from the spotlight, Pinocchio loves to take centre stage when there's a microphone around.

Lord Farquaad

A wicked little man with big ambitions, Lord Farquaad was obsessed with perfection. He banished all fairy-tale creatures from the kingdom of Duloc, since they didn't fit in with his vision of a perfect world. Despite his big chin, page boy hairdo, and vertically challenged physique, Farquaad thought he'd make the perfect king – and desired the perfect bride!

Scheming expression.

Manly frame (with a little help from padded shoulders).

Adjustable table can be lowered and raised according to height of torturer.

Cookie cruelty

Determined to rid himself of every last fairy-tale creature, Farquaad cruelly tortured the Gingerbread Man to find where they were hiding. He was even prepared to remove Gingy's treasured gumdrop buttons!

Farquaad's castle was the biggest bachelor pad ever built – for the smallest occupant! Each night he combed his body hair and dreamt of his perfect bride...

Swishing cape for dramatic exits.

Farquaad's blind date

Lord Farquaad wanted to be king, but the Magic Mirror pointed out that first he had to marry a princess. Available at that time were housemaid blonde, Cinderella; slumbering brunette, Snow White; and a fiery redhead from a dragon-guarded castle – Fiona! For Farquaad there was no competition… Fiona was his perfect pick!

The Magic Mirror had dealt with many vain tyrants, but Farquaad really took the biscuit!

Fun with Thelonius!

Thelonius was Farquaad's head henchman. Here are his magical tips for tip-top torture!

• Intimidate at all times. If your Magic Mirror gets lippy, scare him into silence by smashing a similar shiny object.

• Don't be squeamish. If that Gingerbread Man won't talk – dunk him in milk!

• Don't mix business with pleasure – it's bad manners to eat someone you've just tortured.

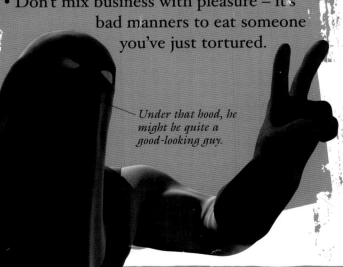

Under that hood, he might be quite a good-looking guy.

Choosing a champion

Freeing Fiona was a dangerous mission. Farquaad offered Shrek his swamp back if he agreed to rescue her. Of course, Shrek could have died while trying, but that's a sacrifice Farquaad was willing to make!

Even after he's met his doom, Farquaad's vanity lives on. A massive gravestone is erected, showing him in heroic battle against an enormous dragon. As if!

Duloc

At the edge of a giant cornfield stood the city of Duloc – the fortress home of Lord Farquaad. Like the man himself, it was insanely neat and orderly. The trees were clipped into perfect cones... the buildings were smart and spotless... cheery music was piped through speakers... souvenir booths were filled with figurines of Lord Farquaad... In fact, it was just like living in a theme park – but without any of the fun rides!

Residents of Duloc always formed orderly lines with the help of ropes and bollards... but ogres don't believe in queueing!

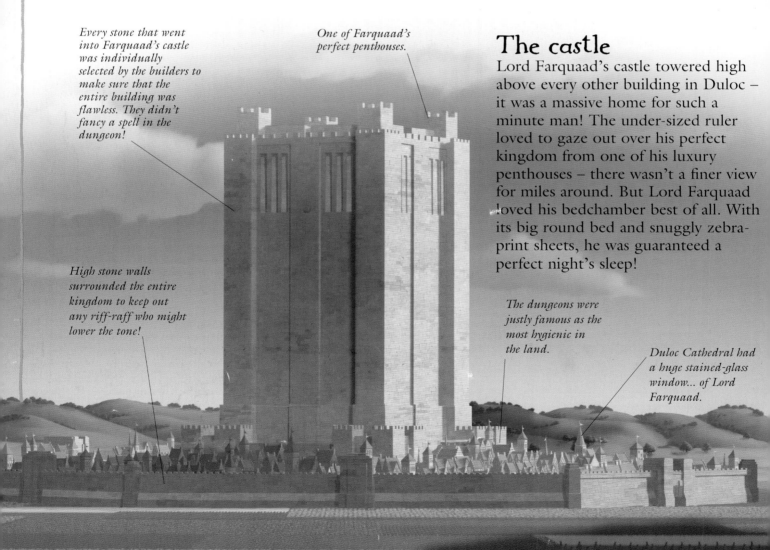

Every stone that went into Farquaad's castle was individually selected by the builders to make sure that the entire building was flawless. They didn't fancy a spell in the dungeon!

One of Farquaad's perfect penthouses.

High stone walls surrounded the entire kingdom to keep out any riff-raff who might lower the tone!

The dungeons were justly famous as the most hygienic in the land.

Duloc Cathedral had a huge stained-glass window... of Lord Farquaad.

The castle

Lord Farquaad's castle towered high above every other building in Duloc – it was a massive home for such a minute man! The under-sized ruler loved to gaze out over his perfect kingdom from one of his luxury penthouses – there wasn't a finer view for miles around. But Lord Farquaad loved his bedchamber best of all. With its big round bed and snuggly zebra-print sheets, he was guaranteed a perfect night's sleep!

Beautiful buildings

All the buildings in Duloc were kept spotlessly clean. That's because armed guards helpfully reminded the peasants to wash them carefully each hour, on the hour! Each blade of grass in the beautiful gardens was snipped by hand!

Turnstile trauma

Just like the theme park it resembled, to get into Duloc you had to walk through the turnstiles. But if you've got four legs, that's not so easy! Donkey somehow squeezed his whole body inside the turnstile – which spun him around and spat him out on the ground!

The rules of Duloc

All visitors to Duloc were met with this single scintillating song...

Welcome to Duloc, such a perfect town
Here we have some rules
Let us lay them down
Don't make waves, stay in line
And we'll get along fine!
Please keep off the grass
Shine your shoes, wipe your... face
Duloc is... Duloc is...
DULOC IS A
PERFECT PLACE!

WELCOME TO
DULOC

Dragon

Charged with guarding Princess Fiona within her castle prison, Dragon lived a lonely life. That was until she met dashing Donkey and the unlikely pair fell in love. Dragon may be fiery but she is also tender-hearted and it's not long before the lovey-dovey couple hear the flutter of dragon-winged dronkeys...

Dragon's wings are powerful.

Dragon never forgets to put on her lipstick – you never know when the donkey of your dreams might appear!

You're fired!

With so few visitors calling at the castle – and since those that did were all boring old knights who had come to do battle with her – it was no wonder that Dragon got crabby. Convinced that the world was out to get her, her policy was to incinerate visitors first and ask questions later – that's until a small, nervous donkey melted her heart!

Powerful throwing arms make the winter knights fly by.

Huge clawed feet for squashing the strongest armour

When Donkey was caught by Dragon he tried to flatter his way out of trouble! The scaly lady took his compliments to heart – and lost her heart to him!

Dragon's love tips

• Line your lair with gold and gemstones – they set off the gleam in your eyes!

• Keep your teeth white and sparkly by flossing regularly!

• There's nothing like lighting a gothic candelabra with your fiery breath to create a romantic atmosphere for you and your beast of burden!

Giant, whip-like tail can smash through solid stone.

A royal pardon–me!

When Fiona needed to be rescued from Farquaad's grasp, Donkey and Dragon fly through Duloc Cathedral's stained glass window! As an encore, Dragon swallowed Farquaad whole – but burped back up his crown!

Dronkeys

Dragon and Donkey are proud parents to their five little fire-breathing dronkeys. But as with all little ones they sometimes need a bit of guidance. What parent hasn't had to tell their son to stop roasting marshmallows on his sister's head?

Strange Enchantment

By night one way, by day another,
This shall be the norm.
Until you find true love's first kiss
And then take love's true form.

This terrible curse was put on Fiona when she was just a little girl. While she was fair and beautiful by day, when the sun set she became a green ogress! Her parents sent her away so that a prince might some day rescue her, fall in love, and kiss her to break the spell.

The trouble with true love is that it can be unpredictable. It's like eating weedrat – who would have thought that something so gross could taste so good? And who would ever think that a big ogre could be so truly lovely? Why… Fiona would!

Putting his hoof in it!

Donkey's choice of words when he first saw the ogress Fiona was unfortunate…

• 'Oh my God, you ate the princess!'

• 'I *told* Shrek those rats were a bad idea!'

• 'You're not that ugly…Well, OK, I'm not going to lie. You ARE ugly…!'

Donkey is not famed for his silver tongue.

Can't face the face

Fiona hated the way she looked at night – she thought she was a horrible, ugly beast. She knew that princesses come in different shapes and sizes but she'd never seen one that looked like an ogress.

No love lost

Fiona believed that marrying Lord Farquaad quickly would break the curse that she had lived with all her life. Farquaad took her speed for love but really Fiona couldn't stand the little lord. She just wanted a kiss from him so that she could finally kiss goodbye to ogress Fiona.

Highs and lows

Unlike their wedding cake decorations, Fiona and Farquaad were not made for each other. They were an odd couple but, most importantly, Fiona was not in love with Farquaad.

White icing wedding dress.

When Shrek kissed Fiona and broke the spell, Fiona took true love's form at last… the form of an ogress!

Announcement

Farquaad's perfect wedding to his pretty princess didn't go quite as he had planned…

DAILY ✦ DULOC

ROYAL WEDDING SHOCKER

It was a right royal disaster for Lord Farquaad today when he accidentally married an OGRESS and then got eaten by a DRAGON!

IN FRONT OF a large crowd of admiring well-wishers (the penalty for non-attendance was death), Lord Farquaad believed he was about to marry the beautiful Princess Fiona – but this was far from a perfect wedding!

Things started to go wrong when notorious ogre SHREK burst into the cathedral objecting to the marriage. But they soon grew worse for Farquaad as his new bride turned into a GREEN ogress, much to the startled Shrek's delight.

THE NEW KING tried to banish both ogres, but was interrupted by a giant dragon crashing through the stained-glass window and swallowing him up in

THE DRAGON'S DRIVER, Donkey, observed, 'Celebrity marriages – they never last do they?' Fiona is soon to marry again – to Shrek. It is believed they will be living happily ever after.

Just Married

Contented smile.

Donkey was hoping that the quest he shared with Shrek would have a happy ending – and it certainly did! With Lord Farquaad out of the way, Shrek and Fiona got married in the swamp. They invited everyone in Duloc and had an amazing party before setting off on a honeymoon neither of them would ever forget!

Love blossoms

A party in a swamp may not be everyone's idea of a dream wedding, but for ogres it's the perfect choice! Shrek remembered Donkey's advice on romance, and had the whole swamp festooned with fabulous flowers.

A fairy turned an onion into a fine wedding carriage and turned the Three Blind Mice into white chargers and a driver!

Honeymoon and beyond!

Fiona and Shrek had a wonderful honeymoon – they frolicked in the sea, stayed in a gingerbread house, taunted fearful villagers and spent long warm nights in a hot tub of mud! But on their return home, the newlyweds were invited to the Kingdom of Far Far Away, where Fiona's parents – the King and Queen – wished to hold a royal ball in honour of her marriage. Donkey insisted on coming along too, since he'd already missed out on all the honeymoon fun!

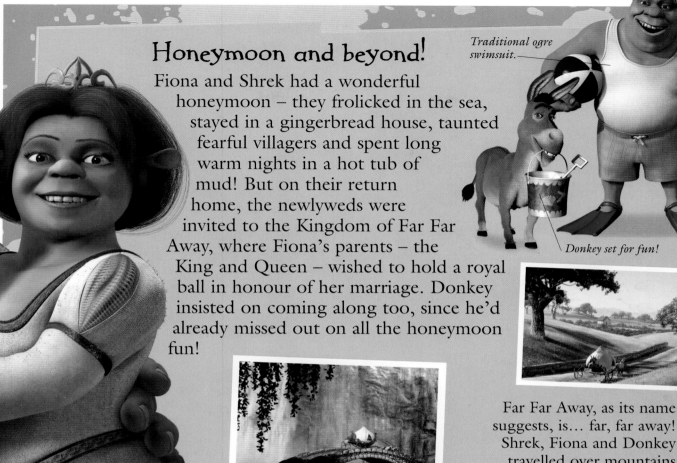

Traditional ogre swimsuit.

Donkey set for fun!

Far Far Away, as its name suggests, is… far, far away! Shrek, Fiona and Donkey travelled over mountains and bridges, through field and vale… and through about 20 different time zones!

Carriage fever

Shrek was nervous on the trip to Far Far Away. He was worried that the King and Queen would never accept an ogre as their son-in-law. To make matters worse, Donkey soon got bored by the long journey. He played I Spy, kept asking 'Are we there yet?' and made lots of annoying POP noises!

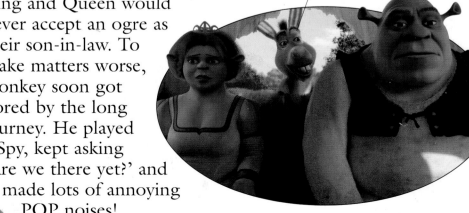

Long, difficult journeys are not made easier by hyperactive donkeys.

Shrek's World

Since his days in the swamp, Shrek has certainly covered a lot of ground. Whether it's driving to Far Far Away in an onion or taking a boat to Worcestershire Academy, Shrek usually has his animal friends with him. Well, almost always. His honeymoon was an ogre-only event.

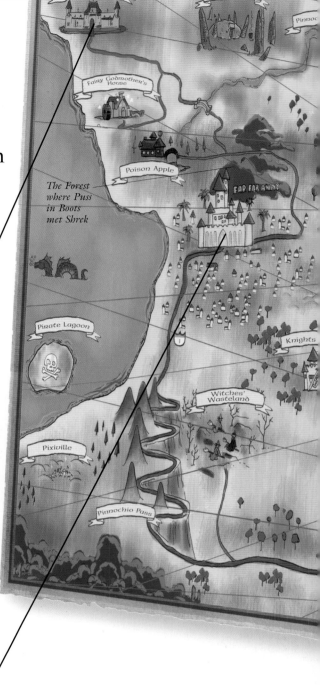

Worcestershire Academy

Situated high on a hilltop, Shrek travelled to Worcestershire Academy to seek Artie, the next heir to the Far Far Away throne. It may be medieval but it's is pretty much like any other school with jocks, geeks and endless lunch lines.

Far Far Away

An exotic land of champagne wishes and caviar dreams, it's said that the streets are paved with gold. This is not strictly true; they're actually made of a mixture of cobblestones and cement. Far Far Away is 200 miles further away than Far Away – and that's not easy to say!

Shrek's swamp

To many, a swamp would be a horrible place to live, but Shrek was happy there. Swapping the delights of giant slugs for a spotless city miles away was more of a difficult decision than it may seem.

Honeymoon Hotel has a private beach where the newlyweds can enjoy the start of their lives together.

Far Far Away

Some say that Hollywood is the place where fairy-tales can come true... but in a kingdom where fairy-tales are real, Far Far Away is the place where dreams can come true! All the fairy-tale princes and princesses flock here to live happily ever after in luxury, making the most of their celebrity status.

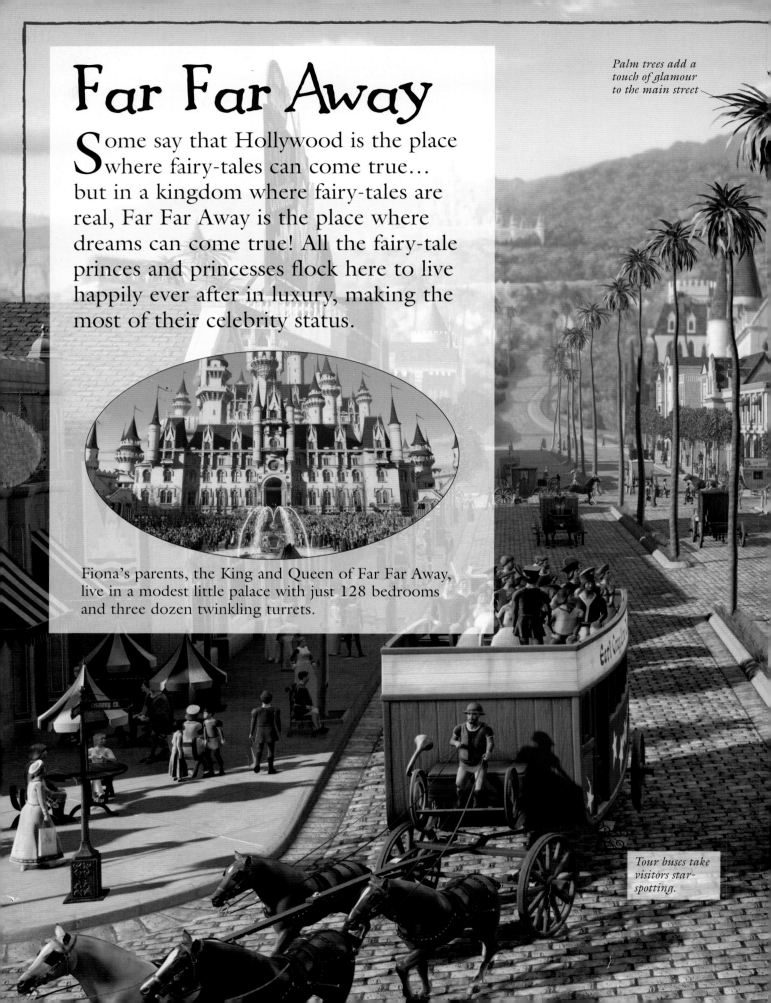

Fiona's parents, the King and Queen of Far Far Away, live in a modest little palace with just 128 bedrooms and three dozen twinkling turrets.

Palm trees add a touch of glamour to the main street

Tour buses take visitors star-spotting.

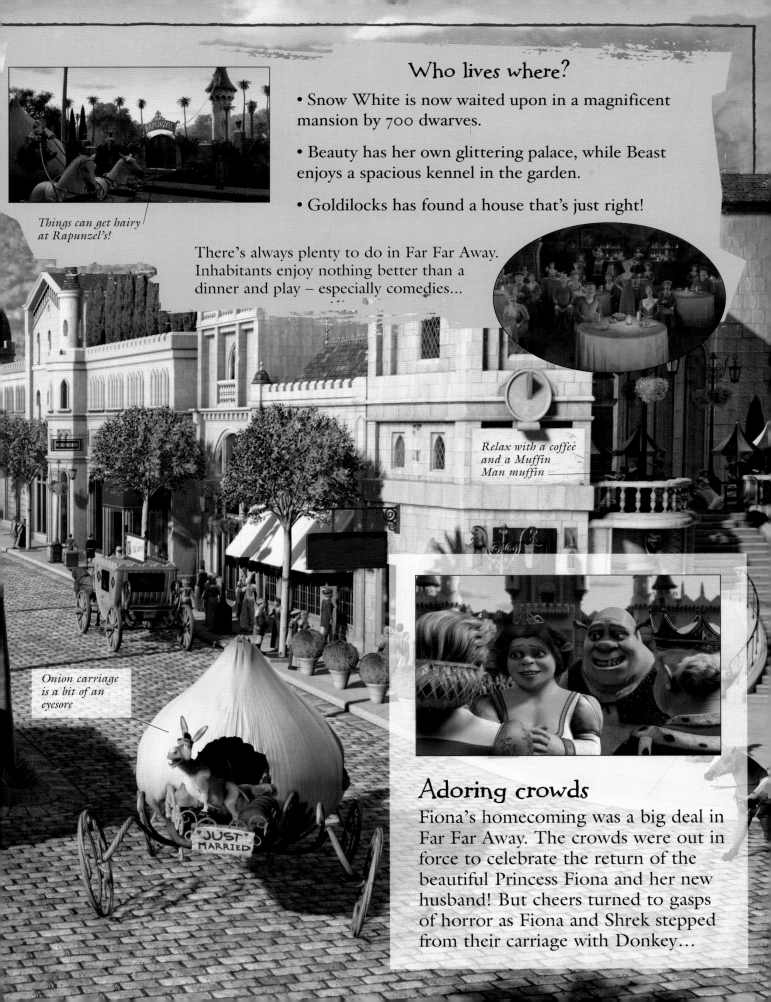

Who lives where?

• Snow White is now waited upon in a magnificent mansion by 700 dwarves.

• Beauty has her own glittering palace, while Beast enjoys a spacious kennel in the garden.

• Goldilocks has found a house that's just right!

Things can get hairy at Rapunzel's!

There's always plenty to do in Far Far Away. Inhabitants enjoy nothing better than a dinner and play – especially comedies...

Relax with a coffee and a Muffin Man muffin

Onion carriage is a bit of an eyesore

JUST MARRIED

Adoring crowds

Fiona's homecoming was a big deal in Far Far Away. The crowds were out in force to celebrate the return of the beautiful Princess Fiona and her new husband! But cheers turned to gasps of horror as Fiona and Shrek stepped from their carriage with Donkey...

Heads of State

Fiona's parents, King Harold and Queen Lillian, are rulers of the Kingdom of Far Far Away. When they locked their daughter away in a tower, they always assumed a handsome prince would rescue her. After many years, they were surprised when their daughter turned up, not only in the company of an ogre – but looking like one too! They soon realised that beauty is in the eye of the beholder.

The king's secret revealed. When Harold deflected a blast from Fairy Godmother's wand, he changed back to that lily pad lounger.

King Harold

The King was shocked that Fiona chose to marry an ogre, and made no secret of his dislike for Shrek. What nobody knew was that the king made a secret deal with Fairy Godmother a long time ago and things didn't go according to plan...

Regal crown set with sapphires.

The royal goatee – king of beards.

Ermine trim paw-stitched by mouse tailors.

Sumptuous royal robes.

Dinner disaster

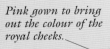

Harold and Lillian laid on a special dinner to welcome Shrek and Fiona, but Shrek wasn't used to royal manners. At dinner, he slurped down the snails with their shells still on. He drank the water from the finger bowls thinking it was soup and then accidentally swallowed a spoon before coughing it back up at high speed. His ogre ways offended King Harold and upset Fiona… but at least Donkey was happy – the food was great!

Lillian didn't have to kiss many frogs before she found her prince. But whether Harold was draped in royal robes or pondweed, Lillian only had eyes for him.

Delicate golden crown studded with royal rubies.

Far, far away look in the royal eyes at all times.

Solid gold stitching.

Queen Lillian

The Queen believes in the power of true love – and is not judging by first appearances. While Shrek is certainly no handsome prince, she tried to make the best of things since he and her daughter were clearly so happy together. Always polite and understanding, she is a wise and popular ruler.

Pink gown to bring out the colour of the royal cheeks.

Finest elf embroidery.

Fairy Godmother

Every princess comes with a Fairy Godmother... what Fiona didn't realise was that hers was a wicked, ambitious schemer! Always surrounded by burly bodyguards, her motto was 'Happiness is just a teardrop away...' but it's *her* happiness she was thinking of! And she wanted Shrek out of the way for her own selfish reasons!

Perfectly styled hair.

Prim glasses convey 'professional' image to clients.

Delicate magic wand for casting sensitive spells.

Flinty fairy

According to the Fairy Godmother, Ogres are not allowed 'happy ever afters'. She believed that Shrek should slope off back to the swamp by himself and let her clean up the 'mess' he'd made of Princess Fiona's life!

Fairy Godmother's appetite was legendary. When she told her son she could eat him all up, she *may* not have been kidding!

Fairy favourite foods

The 'abracadabra diva' always pigged out at times of stress...

• She secretly loved a trip down to Friar's Fat Boy, the medieval drive-through!

• Her favourite order was a Renaissance Wrap and chilli rings... but hold the mayo!

• Her top dessert was anything deep fried and covered in chocolate!

Gossamer fairy wings reinforced to carry great weight.

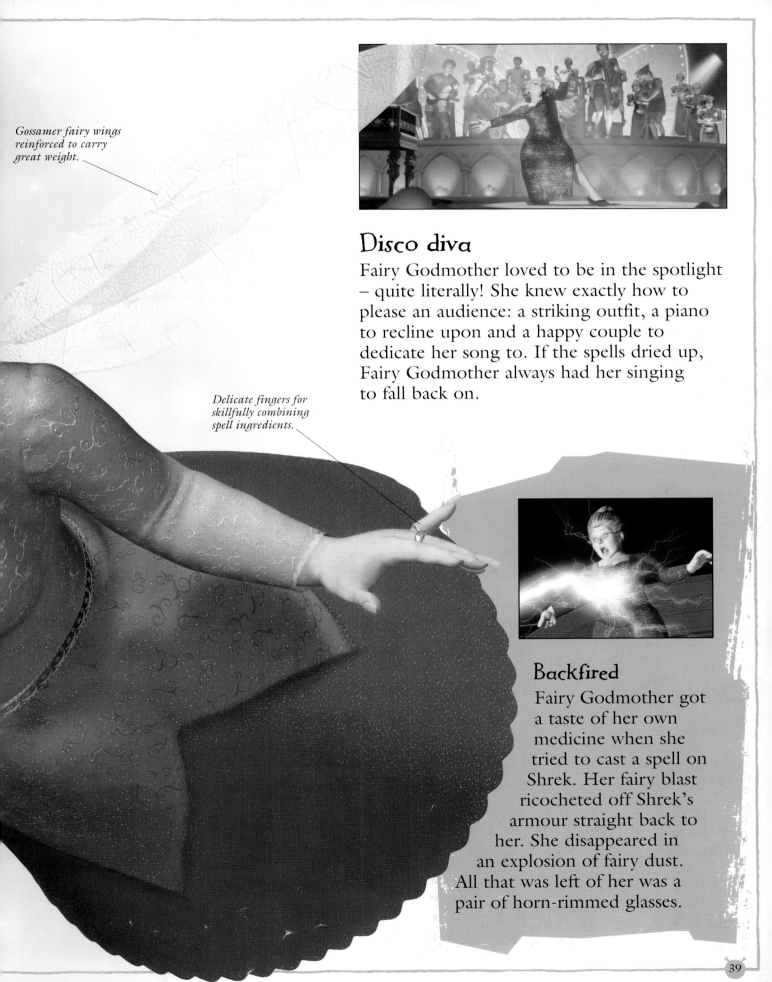

Disco diva

Fairy Godmother loved to be in the spotlight – quite literally! She knew exactly how to please an audience: a striking outfit, a piano to recline upon and a happy couple to dedicate her song to. If the spells dried up, Fairy Godmother always had her singing to fall back on.

Delicate fingers for skillfully combining spell ingredients.

Backfired

Fairy Godmother got a taste of her own medicine when she tried to cast a spell on Shrek. Her fairy blast ricocheted off Shrek's armour straight back to her. She disappeared in an explosion of fairy dust. All that was left of her was a pair of horn-rimmed glasses.

Perfectly styled natural blond mane.

Prince Charming

Handsome, vain and spoilt, Prince Charming is Fairy Godmother's brattish son. He trusted his mother when she said that one day he would be king – and rather than surrender his dreams, Charming embarks on a course of action that will have far-far-reaching effects on Far Far Away...

Puffed out chest.

Mix-up!

Charming entered the castle where Fiona was held once Dragon moved out. However, the Big Bad Wolf had taken Fiona's place!

Charmed tights for wrinkle-free leg look.

Pleasingly expensive golden trim.

Shapely boots show off even shaplier ankle.

Mummy's boy

Just a spoiled, overgrown child at heart, Charming worshipped his mother. She indulged his every whim from Medieval Meals to beautiful princesses. Even though Fairy Godmother is no longer around, Charming will always be 'Mummy's Little Angel'.

How to be charming

Charming's top tips for charming the ladies...

• When choosing a hat, pick a colour that really brings out your razzle-dazzle!

• Call your girl 'Muffin Cake' or 'Kitten Whiskers' – she'll totally respect you for it!

• Cherry flavoured lip-glitter is the mark of a true man!

• The only good Fuzzy Navel is the cocktail – so clean *your* belly button twice a day!

Rebel Raiser

Charming is determined to tell the other side of the fairy-tale – the side of the losers. And if he happens to become King of Far Far Away at the same time then that will do very nicely too.

The world's a stage

Charming hates Shrek for beating him out of being the king of Far Far Away. He writes his own stage play, 'It's a Happily Ever After After All!', which tells his story the way he dreams it could be. In it, Charming plans to slay Shrek in battle and win the crown.

Charming keeps a signed photo of his mum on his mirror for inspiration.

Putting on his show in run-down theatres, Charming stages battles with an ogre-stand-in – but dreams of getting Shrek for real!

Always judge a man by what he drinks.

The Poison Apple

There are some places in Far Far Away that law-abiding folk should steer well clear of... and The Poison Apple pub is one of them! You'll find no airy-fairy tale characters here – only wicked rogues and scoundrels. If you're looking for a fight, a mug of ale in bad company, or even a villain for hire, The Poison Apple is the only place to come!

This singing witch, accompanied by Captain Hook on piano, is popular with the regulars at The Poison Apple.

The other ugly stepsister

The Poison Apple's number one barmaid is Mabel, one of Cinderella's ugly stepsisters. Some say she looks like a lumberjack in a dress! Her sister Doris used to pull the pints but now it's Mabel who gives Charming a Fuzzy Navel.

Sinister forest location for added atmosphere.

Back when King Harold wanted to get rid of Shrek, he visited The Poison Apple to make a deal with Puss In Boots.

Wicked Witch.

Little Red
Riding Hood.

The pirate hospital ran out
of hooks so this pirate had to
be fitted with a spoon.

Evil tree.

Paying regulars

• **Captain Hook** doesn't let his
*hand*icap stop him playing piano!

• If you can't see the wood for the
trees that drink here, ask them to
move... but you'd better ask nicely!

• Many **pirates** linger here, busy
swapping tall tales and treasure
trails, me hearty!

• The **Headless Horseman** likes
to throw a drink down his neck!

Pub brawls

The customers who sup at The Poison Apple
often get a raw deal in life. Rumplestiltskin
doesn't get his firstborn. The Puppet Master's
wooden puppet leaves him all alone. Charming
convinces this rabble of losers to join him and
fight for their right to a 'happy ever after'.
Unfortunately fairy-tale ale and high spirits can
sometimes get out of hand.

Riding the bucking
bronco is Cyclops's
favourite pastime.
However, the pub's
doorman might be
better to spend his
time stopping
undesirables like
Charming from
entering the pub.

Puss In Boots

He is a fierce feline – an adventurer for hire. He's an acrobatic cat with a smooth Spanish accent, fearless and unbeatable in combat – unless he gets a furball! His name is… Puss In Boots! Offered a bag of gold in exchange for 'taking care' of Shrek, Puss confidently accepts. His encounter with Shrek doesn't go to plan, and as a result the two become allies. Shrek soon learns that Puss can be a canny cat to have around!

Should his dazzling battle skills and smooth Spanish charm ever fail him, Puss has another way to get what he wants – he plays the helpless, wide-eyed kitty. Works every time!

Cold steel.

The cat and the donkey

Donkey is cross when Shrek agrees to Puss sharing their adventures – he feels the feisty feline is muscling in on his job as Shrek's best friend. But once the two loyal animals stop competing for Shrek's affections, they learn that they can *both* make a first rate ogre-support team – by working together!

The Puss of myth and song

Puss In Boots has a memorable way with words… Here are just a few of his top-quality quotes!

• 'Ha! ha! Fear me… if you DARE! HISSSSS!'

• 'Now, ye ogre, pray for mercy from… Puss In Boots!'

• 'The winds of fate have blown on my destiny.'

• 'For once, I must agree with the beast of burden.'

• 'It's Puss, the talking gato!'

A bargain struck

After a battle in which Puss nearly loses one of his nine stylish lives, the dashing cat decides he may have misjudged the ogre. He tells Shrek, 'On my honour, I am obliged to accompany you until I have saved your life as you have spared me mine.'

Stylish black hat with primrose yellow plume.

Cape for full swashbuckling effect.

Special 'kitty customised' miniature rapier.

Buccaneering belt.

Striped tail for perfect poise and balance.

Dashing leather boots (can be leapt right out of in an emergency).

Puss certainly has a way with the female felines. Trouble is, he seems to be deeply in love with every cat he meets. It's not surprising that he leaves a trail of catfights behind him.

Potion Factory

In the middle of an enchanted glade stood Fairy Godmother's incredible potion factory. From the vast array of colourful ingredients that were kept there, she conjured her world-famous potions… But did her 'Happily Ever After' spell work for Shrek?

Giant wheel helped turn a conveyor belt – potion in motion!

To ensure even mixing, an elfin centrifuge put ingredients in a spin!

Catwalk for overseeing elves at work.

Potions weren't made from magic alone – there was plenty of complex chemistry used too!

Ingredients were together in huge

Thatched factory

Fairy Godmother's Potion Factory appeared to be a picturesque cottage but if you looked up you could see the large chimneys billowing out smoke from the magical mixtures.

Each bottle was filed alphabetically.

As a safety precaution, powerful potions were kept behind glass.

The Potion Storage Room contained thousands of potions.

Ingredients travelled on rails to the vats as required.

Magical map of the kingdom helped elves keep track of potion deliveries.

Bad for your elf!

The potions required very careful handling and the elfin workers wore special protective suits. Security elves were employed to guard the potions from any would-be thieves.

Most popular potions
Fairy Godmother's top-selling spells:

• Warm Spell Potion – guaranteed to make the coldest day sunny and bright!

• Elfa Seltzer – if you're feeling flat, a swig of this woulmake you as perky as a pixie!

• Oinkment – shrinks your stomach when you can't stop pigging out!

Elfa Seltzer

Warm Spell Potion

Oinkment

Transformation!

Thinking that Fiona would be happier if he was handsome and no longer an ogre, Shrek (and Donkey) drank a 'Happily Ever After' potion. Soon, the two of them were magically transformed into magnificent males. But was this *really* the look that Fiona would go for, or did Shrek make a terrible mistake?

Powdered wig.

Change for the better?

Shrek found that with his cute button nose and wavy hair, he was irresistible to women! Donkey agreed that Shrek was easier on the eyes, but *inside* he was still the same cranky, stanky ogre he'd always been!

Much to his delight, Donkey was transformed into a magnificent stallion. He could whinny, preen, gallop and trot like a truly noble steed!

Clothes stolen from a nobleman.

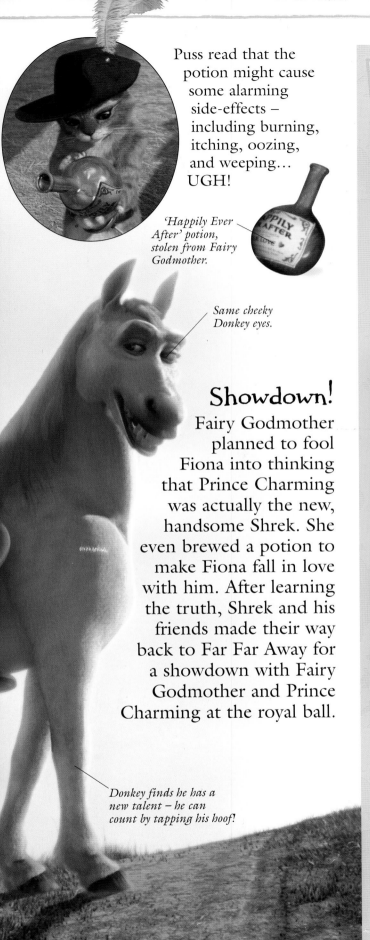

Puss read that the potion might cause some alarming side-effects – including burning, itching, oozing, and weeping… UGH!

'Happily Ever After' potion, stolen from Fairy Godmother.

Same cheeky Donkey eyes.

Showdown!

Fairy Godmother planned to fool Fiona into thinking that Prince Charming was actually the new, handsome Shrek. She even brewed a potion to make Fiona fall in love with him. After learning the truth, Shrek and his friends made their way back to Far Far Away for a showdown with Fairy Godmother and Prince Charming at the royal ball.

Donkey finds he has a new talent – he can count by tapping his hoof!

If Shrek and Fiona kissed before midnight, they would remain in their 'beautiful' forms. But Fiona decided to stop the kiss…

New Couple

Fiona realised that she wanted to be with the man she married and that's a green ogre not a wigged nobleman. The clock chimed midnight and the pair were transformed back to the ogre and ogress that they truly are.

The King is Dead

A statue of the late King in his true amphibian form is erected in the palace garden.

After a number of false alarms King Harold finally passes away leaving Far Far Away in need of a new ruler – and Shrek and Fiona are next in line! The prospect of permanently living a royal life fills Shrek with horror but there's a funeral to get through before he can deal with the challenge of finding an alternative heir to the throne.

A funeral fit for a king

The King's tiny body is placed in a shoebox and the state funeral takes place in the palace grounds. The solemn congregation look on as Queen Lillian gently lowers the coffin onto a lily pad in the pond and says a final farewell to her husband as it drifts away.

As a tribute to the king, a choir of frogs sing as he returns to the pond that was once his home.

Grieving fairy-tale creatures bow their heads in respect.

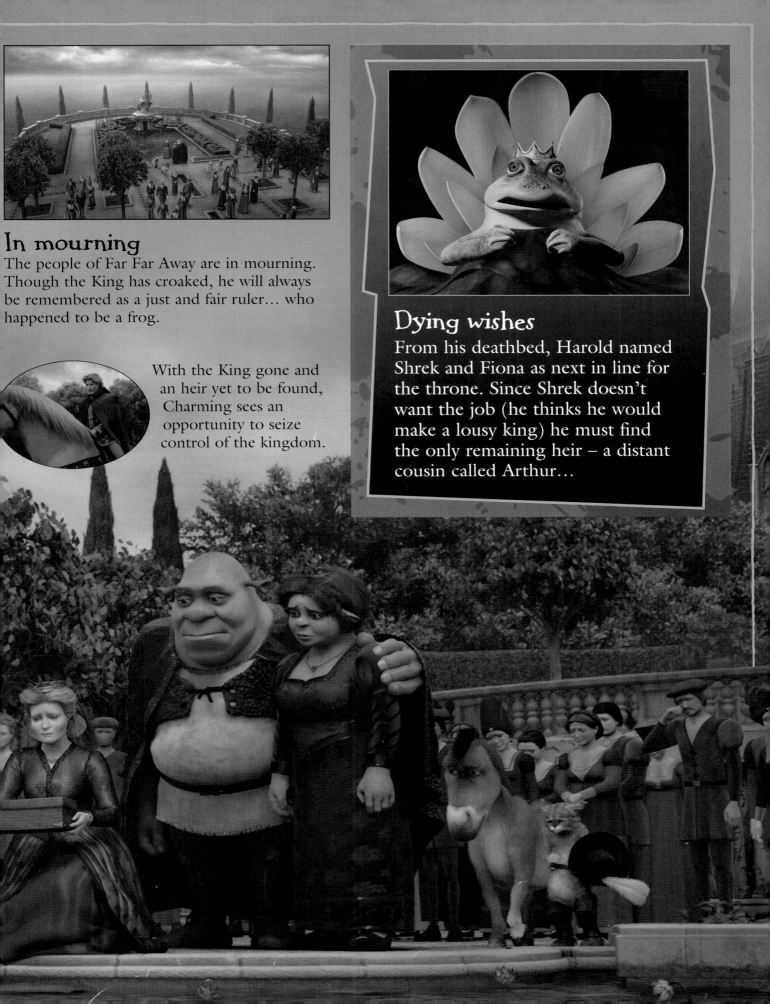

In mourning

The people of Far Far Away are in mourning. Though the King has croaked, he will always be remembered as a just and fair ruler... who happened to be a frog.

With the King gone and an heir yet to be found, Charming sees an opportunity to seize control of the kingdom.

Dying wishes

From his deathbed, Harold named Shrek and Fiona as next in line for the throne. Since Shrek doesn't want the job (he thinks he would make a lousy king) he must find the only remaining heir – a distant cousin called Arthur...

Royal Duties

Shrek and Fiona had to take over royal duties when King Harold became sick. Their days are filled with school visits, knighting ceremonies and boat launches. However, Shrek and Fiona soon find that being king and queen is not all plain sailing.

Decorative birds, bows and berries.

Stiff collar – useful for resting party snacks on.

Purple may be a royal colour but it clashes with Shrek's skin.

Shrek need... wide-fit sh...

Nervous knight

One of Shrek's royal duties is to give a man a knighthood but the ceremony goes horribly wrong when Shrek accidentally stabs the recipient. Even the bravest of men would be nervous at the sight of an ogre approaching with a sword in his hand but it turns out this man had good cause to worry!

How to make an ogre beautiful

Make-up artist to the rich and royal, Raul knows all the tricks of the trade. He's met his toughest subjects yet, though, with Shrek and Fiona. It's so difficult to get ogre green foundation nowadays.

Every great artist needs great tools but Raul's look more like torture devices.

Mascara makes th... eyelashes look lo... and sometimes t... eyes tearier.

Frightening fairy-tale

Fiona hopes that dad-to-be Shrek will remember not to read scary tales to their baby. He manages to scare a whole class with 'Little Red Riding Hood'!

Shrek is used to people crying at the way he looks but not at his storytelling abilities.

Outfits were more comfortable in days gone by.

Fiona doesn't feel pretty in pink.

Fire and water

Ogres and ships do not mix. When Shrek is called on to launch a ship, the event ends with the boat bursting into flames.

Not everyone is pleased Shrek is standing in for King Harold.

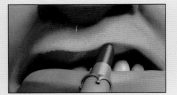

A bold red is a popular lip colour but Shrek is not too happy with this new look.

If you don't have regular pedicures, the circular sander is sometimes called for.

Fiona gets to learn all about the art of corset-wearing: breathe in and pass out.

Finishing touches are important. If the shoe fits (or even if it doesn't), wear it.

Artie

Meet Arthur Pendragon. After Fiona, he is the rightful heir to the throne. Artie is the only person who can unite the land. Unfortunately, he's still at school and most people think he's far more likely to become Mayor of Loserville than the King of Far Far Away!

The hair of an heir.

Worcestershire Academy

Run by Principal Pynchley, Worcestershire Academy is like a medieval school. When Shrek and his pals journey there to find Artie, Shrek's stomach aches and his palms sweat. He didn't enjoy his school days.

Academy tunics must be worn at all times.

Uncertain heir

Lacking in confidence, Artie doesn't think he could ever be a good king. Poor Artie was abandoned at Worcestershire Academy by his father. Artie never heard from his dad again, and has felt like a failure ever since.

Tights damaged in sporting incident.

Artie isn't just quick-thinking – he is fast on his feet too!

It takes Shrek to show Artie that just because people treat you like junk, it doesn't mean that's what you are.

On the road

Cart-driving lessons are a popular choice among pupils at Worcestershire Academy. Students learn the benefits of unleaded hay, the best way to ease up on the reigns and how to change a punctured horseshoe. Pupils that are top of the class get to drive the convertible cart.

A sword fit for a king – but is Artie a fitting contender?

Knight mare

A bold knight rides his steed across the jousting pitch. It is no surprise that Shrek mistakes this handsome, regal-looking figure for Arthur. However, this is Lancelot, the school jock. That's Lancelot, not Peaches, as Artie advises Shrek to call him!

Cheerleading can be tiring when your school's name is as long as Worcestershire Academy. 'Give me a "W", give me an "O"...'

The course of high-school love never did run smooth. These medieval maidens would rather get the black plague than go out with some of the geeks from the Academy.

Gameplay

These lads steer well clear of the sportsfield. They prefer their games to be played out on a board. They regularly miss their weight-training classes. After all, the heaviest thing they'll ever need to throw is a few dice.

Merlin

Suffering from a "level three fatigue" – that's a nervous breakdown to you and me – Merlin used to teach magic at Worcestershire Academy. Now he has retired to the peaceful forest where he lets it all hang out – an airy robe's a must when you break out in itchy rashes at the drop of a pointed hat!

Doubles as tea-cosy.

Glasses help when reading detailed spells.

Well-ventilated robe.

Reluctantly ready to lend hi. friends a helpfu. magical hand.

Extra-long beard is a sign of wisdom (and possibly laziness).

"Cool" socks with sandals look – wizards don't care for fashion!

Lessons learned

Merlin's lessons at Worcestershire Academy were simply magic! Students who attended his classes often won the local spelling bee competitions – to Merlin's great delight and surprise!

Body swap!

Merlin hasn't performed any spells for some time, so when he tries to send Shrek and his friends back to Far Far Away there's one tiny little side-effect. Donkey and Puss swap bodies! Will life ever be the same for either of them?

Sharp tongue

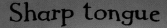

Many mystical, magical words have been spoken softly by this wise wizard. But he's also good at snarling out impeccable insults!

• To Shrek – "Hey, watch it, ya spinach-tinted monkey!"

• To dinner guests – "Freeloading ingrates, honing in on my piece of plenty!"

Spelling it out

Merlin claims to have lost most of his good spells some time ago. Nevertheless, there's magic in the old guy yet! Check out these charms...

Transportation Spell
Alacraticious
Expeditious, a zoomy
zoom zoom.
Let's help our friends
get back, uh... soon!

Swords into Chickens

In the evil villain's den
Take a shiny sword and then
Cluck! Clucky-cluck!
With a little magic luck
We will make of it a
rubber hen!

Calming Spell
I am a river
flow, flow, flow
Angry thoughts wash away
go, go, go!
Buzz, buzzy buzz!
I am a small bee
Soon I shall regain
my tranquility

Evil Trees

These spiky trees are dropped from the witches' broomsticks to scare unsuspecting passers-by in Far Far Away. They find it difficult to branch out from being evil.

Cyclops

Most bouncers need to have eyes in the back of their heads. Cyclops has to make do with one right in the middle of his forehead. Still, Charming knows that this giant will put all his muscle behind his mission to take over Far Far Away.

Evil Queen

A mean pool player, the Evil Queen wants to open a spa in France with many mirrors on the wall.

Puppet Master
The melancholy Puppet Master would like a simple life with no strings attached.

Captain Hook
Resident pianist at The Poison Apple, Captain Hook is all about the music. He even plays his own atmospheric soundtrack when his pirate crew gets into fights.

Headless Horseman
The Headless Horseman is usually calm (he's only ever lost his head once).

Rogues Gallery

Prince Charming picks a motley crew to help in his quest to become the king of Far Far Away. A one-eyed giant, trees with a streak of evil and a pirate who's happy to lend a hook is not everyone's idea of a tremendous team but Charming hopes that their desire to change their own miserable lives will spur them on.

Little Red Riding Hood is suspicious of everyone. Who can blame her? A wolf did pretend to be her grandmother.

Mabel is still haunted by the memory of trying to fit her fat foot into the tiny glass slipper.

Under Attack

Having convinced The Poison Apple customers that they deserve their Happily Ever Afters, Prince Charming sets off to Far Far Away. His airborne army speeds along on broomsticks, dropping Evil Trees as they go.

Witch way?

In downtown, the witches drop the Evil Trees onto the unsuspecting shoppers who run away in fear. The poor people of Far Far Away have just got used to the fact that their king is a frog but walking and talking trees are too much to take!

When you want to make a big impression, arriving by broomstick works every time.

This woman wishes Hook would stop calling her Wendy.

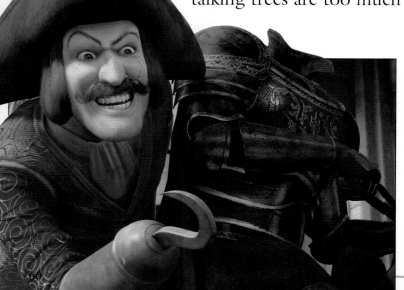

By Hook and by Crook

Captain Hook and his headless honcho immediately make their presence known in Far Far Away. However, Hook seems to be stuck in his own fairy-tale and is convinced this little boy is Peter Pan.

Reinforced broomstick for carrying passengers.

Charming is a real backseat driver.

Evil Trees hang from broomsticks, ready for firing.

Stamp Out
Cyclops removes the stamps from the mail and puts them back in the mailbox. This one-eyed wonder truly knows how to be bad!

Barricades
The fairy-tale creatures block the doors from Charming as he enters the castle. The Three Little Pigs know that no one will be able to blow the castle down but can they stop Charming and his crew in time?

Princess Power

A baby shower is thrown for Princess Fiona to celebrate the pattering of tiny green feet. Little does she realise that her guests will be vital to the future of Far Far Away. For when Prince Charming invades with his army of villains, only these brave women – and their fairy-tale friends – stand in his way!

Dragon's too big to fit inside the palace, but she does drop i on the baby shower to share a little fiery advice – and warn th group of the villains' arrival.

For feisty Fiona, a girly baby shower is not her idea of fun. She can't get excited about maternity dresses and baby pooper scoopers!

Queen's head – useful for headbutting through cell walls.

Snow White gets Fiona a live-in babysitter – a Nanny Dwarf!

Pinocchio loves a good party.

Royal rebels

The princesses think their roles are set in stone. When they are thrown in a cell after trying to escape from Charming their first reaction is to sit and wait to be rescued. But Queen Lillian shows them that they control their destinies. Let battle commence...

Fighting Princesses

Fiona thinks that Rapunzel has been snatched by Charming but it turns out the pair are actually dating. Charming and his little 'kitten whiskers' are quite an item. His opinion of the other princesses is not as high. He wants to see them all scrubbing floors or locked away in terrible towers. But he hadn't bargained on the new, improved princesses...

Rapunzel is the wannabe queen of Far Far Away.

Snow White

Vocally talented Snow White encourages all the forest creatures to flock to her – and attack the Evil Trees.

Cinderella

Cinderella is always cleaning, a habit that dates back to when she slaved away for her stepsisters'. She cleans up in a fight, sweeping up every crumb and crooked guard.

Sleeping Beauty

This Beauty is not just a pretty face. Beauty's sleeping issue has its uses. When a guard chases her, she falls asleep and he trips over her.

Rapunzel

Snow White reveals that Rapunzel isn't a natural blonde. But it seems this icy beauty has other, darker secrets...

Has tattoo of Dopey on arm.

Secretly wears hair extensions.

Beauty rips the hem off her dress so she can do ninja kicks.

Boomerang glass slipper for fighting.

LONDON, NEW YORK, MUNICH,
MELBOURNE, AND DELHI

SENIOR DESIGNER Guy Harvey   **SENIOR EDITOR** Lindsay Kent

DESIGNER Thelma Jane Robb   **PUBLISHING MANAGER** Simon Beecroft

BRAND MANAGER Rob Perry   **CATEGORY PUBLISHER** Alex Allan

DTP DESIGNER Hanna Ländin   **PRODUCTION** Amy Bennett

First published in Great Britain in 2007 by Dorling Kindersley Limited,
80 Strand, London, WC2R 0RL
A Penguin Company

07 08 09 10 11 10 9 8 7 6 5 4 3 2 1

A CIP catalogue record for this book is available from the British Library.

ISBN 978-1-4053-1845-7

Reproduced by Media Development and Printing, UK
Printed and bound by Leo Paper Products Ltd., China

Acknowledgements
Dorling Kindersley would like to thank the following:
Kristy Cox, Corinne Combs, Rhion Magee, and the staff at
DreamWorks Animation L.L.C. for all their help; Roger Harris
for additional artworks; Laura Gilbert for editorial assistance.

Discover more at
www.dk.com